28 Days of Black History
for Little Ones

Small Poems about Unsung Heroes

by Marsha Davenport and Allison Dearstyne

To little ones everywhere to learn and remember Unsung Heroes of Black History!

Table of Contents

Day 1 - Carter G. Woodson
Day 2 - Mo'Ne Davis
Day 3 - Charlotte E. Ray
Day 4 - Josephine St. Pierre Ruffin
Day 5 - Henry "Box" Brown
Day 6 - William Henry Cling
Day 7 - Matthew Henson
Day 8 - Susie King Taylor
Day 9 - Alexander Miles
Day 10 - George Washington Bush
Day 11 - Daniel Hale Williams
Day 12 - Elizabeth Taylor Greenfield
Day 13 - Benjamin Banneker
Day 14 - Annie Malone
Day 15 - Jan Ernst Matzeliger
Day 16 - Sophia Danenberg
Day 17 - James McCune Smith
Day 18 - Emma Azalia Smith Hackley
Day 19 - Clara Brown
Day 20 - Warren Shadd
Day 21 - Elizabeth Jennings Graham
Day 22 - Charlotte Forten
Day 23 - William Carney
Day 24 - Norbert Rillieux
Day 25 - Harriet Powers
Day 26 - George Speck
Day 27 - Ernest Green
Day 28 - Charlotte Hawkins Brown

Day 1 - Carter G. Woodson

Carter G. Woodson realized to most,
Black heroes were a mystery.
So thanks to him, every February
we celebrate Black History!

Day 2 - Mo'Ne Davis

Mo'Ne Davis was the only girl on a Little League Baseball Team. She set new records at thirteen, the All-American Dream.

Day 3 - Charlotte E. Ray

Charlotte E. Ray had quite a career;
Howard U. was her employer.
She disguised her gender to get into law school,
and was the first Black woman lawyer!

Day 4 - Josephine St. Pierre Ruffin

We thank Josephine Ruffin;
she worked, marched and wrote.
And thanks to her efforts, along with others
women were given the vote!

Day 5 - Henry "Box" Brown

Slave Henry "Box" Brown put himself in a crate to be mailed to the North and then when he arrived, he greeted his friends, "How do you do, gentlemen?"

Day 6 - William Henry Cling

Inventor William Henry Cling put emergency brakes inside trains. He also made the first hospital beds so patients could sit up without strain!

Day 7 - Matthew Henson

Explorer Matthew Henson traveled to a frozen land.
He learned from the Natives, and on the North Pole he was the first to stand!

Day 8 - Susie King Taylor

Susie King Taylor was the first Black nurse;
for the Union she faithfully served.
She worked to heal Black soldiers
without the pay that she deserved.

Day 9 - Alexander Miles

Alexander Miles was an inventor of elevator doors that could slide. Their automatic closing made them safe to ride!

Day 10 - George Washington Bush

George Washington Bush was a pioneer who settled in the Northwest.
He built a hotel where he gave free meals and lodging to all of his guests!

Day 11 - Daniel Hale Williams

Daniel Hale Williams operated on a wounded man's open heart. It was the very first time that surgery worked because he was so smart!

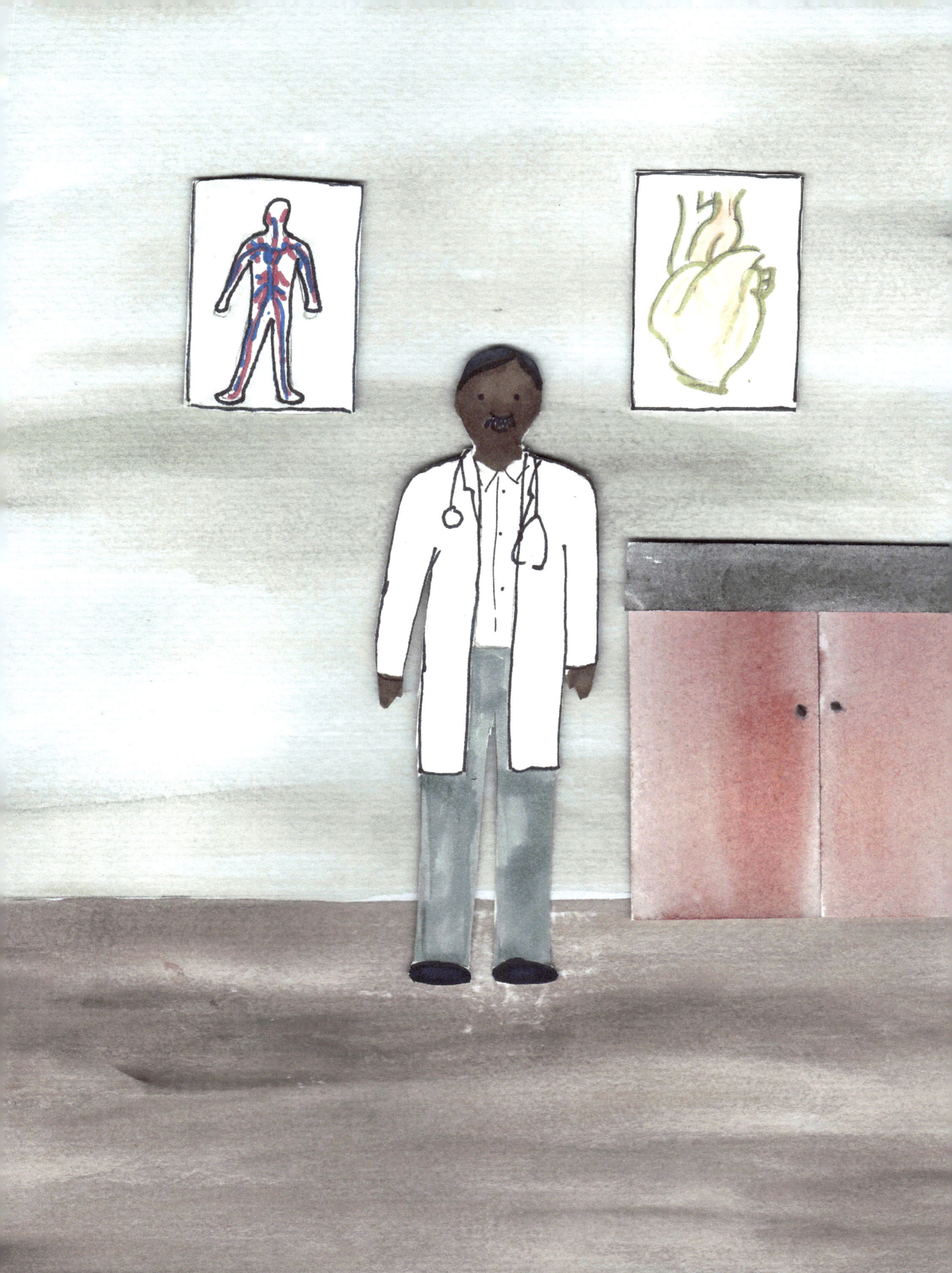

Day 12 - Elizabeth Taylor Greenfield

Talented Elizabeth T. Greenfield
could sing both soprano and bass.
Called the "Black Swan," she traveled the world
singing all over the place!

Day 13 - Benjamin Banneker

Benjamin Banneker was super smart;
by the stars he mapped out D.C.
He wrote guidebooks for farmers
and fishermen at sea!

Day 14 - Annie Malone

Annie Malone saw that there were no products to straighten Black hair. She made a recipe for new products making it easy for proper care!

Day 15 - Jan Ernst Matzeliger

Jan Ernst Matzeliger made a machine for shoe factories to use.
He sped up the process that once took so long attaching soles to shoes!

Day 16 - Sophia Danenberg

Trailblazer Sophia Danenberg went out on a quest.
With stinging lungs and frostbite she reached the top of Everest!

Day 17 - James McCune Smith

James McCune Smith was the first Black American with a medical degree.
He was also the first Black American to open a pharmacy!

Day 18 - Emma Azalia Smith Hackley

We thank Emma A. S. Hackley,
a singer and musician
who taught others about her culture
and made it her whole life's mission!

Day 19 - Clara Brown

Clara Brown was born a slave,
was freed, then traveled west.
In Colorado she gave much;
by giving she was blessed!

Day 20 - Warren Shadd

Warren Shadd is a musician
who was in a jazz band;
he made a new piano
and owns his special brand!

Day 21 - Elizabeth Jennings Graham

Elizabeth J. Graham got kicked off a trolley all because of her race.
She went to court to set things right and she won the case!

Day 22 - Charlotte Forten

Charlotte Forten kept a diary of her days in the Civil War. She taught ex-slaves, and through her we learn education can open a door!

Day 23 - William Carney

Sergeant William Carney in the Civil War was found waving the flag, exclaiming with pride, "The flag never touched the ground!"

Day 24 - Norbert Rillieux

Norbert Rillieux was an engineer who created a new machine that improved the way sugar was made to be safe, pure and clean!

Day 25 - Harriet Powers

Harriet Powers was born a slave and through quilting did her part to tell stories of local legends and the Bible through her art!

Day 26 - George Speck

Chef George Speck had a picky customer
who didn't like thick fries.
George made the first chips when he cut them so thin
best potatoes he ever tried!

Day 27 - Ernest Green

Ernest Green went to a White high school, and helped them to integrate.
He was the very first one of the "Little Rock Nine" to go on to graduate!

Day 28 - Charlotte Hawkins Brown

Teacher Charlotte "Lottie" H. Brown raised money for her school. She taught her students that they would do well to follow the Golden Rule!

Bibliography

"A Student Remembers." *Charlotte Hawkins Brown Museum.* North Carolina Historic Sites. 06 Oct. 2015. Web. 07 Aug. 2018.

African American Registry.org editors. "Josephine Ruffin, activist, philanthropist, and newspaper publisher." *AAREG.* Web. 04 Jan. 2019.

Biography.com Editors. "Henry "Box" Brown Biography." The Biography.com website. A&E Television Networks. 22 Aug. 2019. Web. 11 Jan. 2020.

BlackInventor.com editors. "George Crum: Inventor of Potato Chips." *BlackInventors.com.* Famous Black Inventors: A Rich Heritage Gives Way to Modern Ingenuity. Web. 09 Jan. 2019.

Biography.com editors. "Charlotte Hawkins Brown Biography." *The Biography.com website.* A&E Television Networks. 26 Sep. 2015. Web. 07 Aug. 2018.

Biography.com editors. "Clara Brown Biography." *The Biography.com website.* A&E Television Networks. 21 Sep. 2015. Web. 24 Jun. 2018

Biography.com editors. "Charlotte Forten Biography." *The Biography.com website.* A&E Television Networks. 01 Apr. 2014. Web. 10 Aug. 2018.

Biography.com editors. "Elizabeth Jennings Graham Biography." *The Biography.com website.* A&E Television Networks. 20 Oct. 2015. Web. 16 Aug. 2018.

Biography.com editors. "Elizabeth Taylor Greenfield Biography." *The Biography.com website.* A&E Television Networks. 01 Apr. 2014. Web. 09 Sep. 2018.

Biography.com editors. "Matthew Henson Biography." *The Biography.com website*. A&E Television Networks. 02 Apr. 2014. Web. 12 Dec. 2018.

Brenton, Felix. "Danenberg, Sophia (1972-). *BlackPast.org.* Remembered & Reclaimed. Web. 29 Dec. 2018.

Cabiao, Howard. "Ray, Charlotte E." *BlackPast.org.* Remembered and Reclaimed. 2017. Web. 12 Aug. 2018

"Harriet Powers (1837-1911)." *americanartgallery.org.* Web. 14 Jan. 2020.

Helm, Matt. "Carney, William H. (1840-1908)." *BlackPast.org.* Remembered and Reclaimed. 2017. Web. 26 Sep. 2018

Jenkins, Willard. "The First African-American Piano Manufacturer." *A Blog Supreme from NPR Jazz.* National Public Radio. 07 May 2014. Web. 13 Jan. 2019.

"Madame Emma Azalia Smith Hackley." *Historic Elmwood Cemetery & Foundation.* Where Detroit's History Endures. Web. 15 Oct. 2018

McHugh, Catherine. "Who Was Charlotte E. Ray?" *The Biography.com website*. A&E Television Networks. 21 Sep. 2015. Web. 24 Jun. 2018.

Mitchell, Adam. "Conversation with Sophia Danenberg: First African American to Climb Everest." *Melanin Base Camp.* 31 Jan. 2018. Web. 29 Dec. 2018.

MyBlackHistory.net editors. "Alexander Miles." *MyBlackHistory.net.* Web. 14 Dec. 2018.

MyBlackHistory.net editors. "Norbert Rillieux." *MyBlackHistory.net.* Web. 14 Dec. 2018.

MyBlackHistory.net editors. "Daniel Hale Williams." *MyBlackHistory.net.* Web. 14 Dec. 2018.

Olsen, Winnifred and Shanna Stevenson. "George Bush (1789?-1863)." blackpast.org. 19 Jan. 2007. Web. 3 Dec. 2019.

"Only a Teacher: Charlotte Forten." *PBS.org,* WETA. Web. 10 Aug. 2018

Peterson, Heather. "Hackley, Emma Azalia (1867-1922)." *BlackPast.org.* Remembered and Reclaimed. Web. 15 Oct. 2018.

Rogers, J.A. *World's Great Men of Color, Volume II.* Macmillan Publishing, 1972.

"Susie Baker King Taylor." *Battlefields.org.* American Battlefield Trust. Web. 14 Jan. 2020.

"Susie King Taylor." *nps.gov.* National Park Service. 30 Mar. 2019. Web. 14 Jan. 2020.

"Warren M. Shadd: About." ShaddPianos.com. Web. 13 Jan. 2019.

Wikipedia contributors. "Benjamin Banneker." *Wikipedia, The Free Encyclopedia.* Wikipedia, The Free Encyclopedia, 12 Dec. 2018. Web. 13 Dec. 2018.

Wikipedia contributors. "Clara Brown." *Wikipedia, The Free Encyclopedia.* Wikipedia, The Free Encyclopedia, 8 May. 2018. Web. 24 Jun. 2018.

Wikipedia contributors. "Henry Box Brown." *Wikipedia, The Free Encyclopedia*. Wikipedia, The Free Encyclopedia, 8 Jan. 2020. Web. 11 Jan. 2020.

Wikipedia contributors. "George Washington Bush." *Wikipedia, The Free Encyclopedia*. Wikipedia, The Free Encyclopedia, 14 Nov. 2019. Web. 1 Dec. 2019.

Wikipedia contributors. "William Harvey Carney." *Wikipedia, The Free Encyclopedia*. Wikipedia, The Free Encyclopedia, 6 Sep. 2018. Web. 27 Sep. 2018.

Wikipedia contributors. "William Henry Cling." *Wikipedia, The Free Encyclopedia*. Wikipedia, The Free Encyclopedia, 18 Oct. 2017. Web. 24 Sep. 2018

Wikipedia contributors. "George Crum." *Wikipedia, The Free Encyclopedia*. Wikipedia, The Free Encyclopedia, 9 Jan. 2019. Web. 9 Jan. 2019.

Wikipedia contributors. "Sophia Danenberg." *Wikipedia, The Free Encyclopedia*. Wikipedia, The Free Encyclopedia, 22 Dec. 2017. Web. 29 Dec. 2018.

Wikipedia contributors. "Mo'ne Davis." *Wikipedia, The Free Encyclopedia*. Wikipedia, The Free Encyclopedia, 22 Nov. 2018. Web. 10 Jan. 2019."

Wikipedia contributors. "Ernest Green." *Wikipedia, The Free Encyclopedia*. Wikipedia, The Free Encyclopedia, 13 Jan. 2019. Web. 14 Jan. 2019.

Wikipedia contributors. "Emma Azalia Hackley." *Wikipedia, The Free Encyclopedia*. Wikipedia, The Free Encyclopedia, 18 Jan. 2018. Web. 15 Oct. 2018.

Wikipedia contributors. "Matthew Henson." *Wikipedia, The Free Encyclopedia*. Wikipedia, The Free Encyclopedia, 29 Nov. 2018. Web. 13 Dec. 2018.

Wikipedia contributors. "Annie Malone." *Wikipedia, The Free Encyclopedia*. Wikipedia, The Free Encyclopedia, 30 Nov. 2018. Web. 13 Dec. 2018.

Wikipedia contributors. "Jan Ernst Matzeliger." *Wikipedia, The Free Encyclopedia*. Wikipedia, The Free Encyclopedia, 4 Dec. 2018. Web. 7 Dec. 2018.

Wikipedia contributors. "Harriet Powers." *Wikipedia, The Free Encyclopedia*. Wikipedia, The Free Encyclopedia, 9 Jan. 2020. Web. 14 Jan. 2020.

Wikipedia contributors. "James McCune Smith." *Wikipedia, The Free Encyclopedia*. Wikipedia, The Free Encyclopedia, 1 Dec. 2018. Web. 6 Dec. 2018.

Wikipedia contributors. "Susie Taylor." *Wikipedia, The Free Encyclopedia*. Wikipedia, The Free Encyclopedia, 21 Oct. 2019. Web. 14 Jan. 2020.

Wikipedia contributors. "Norbert Rillieux." *Wikipedia, The Free Encyclopedia*. Wikipedia, The Free Encyclopedia, 22 Jun. 2018. Web. 16 Dec. 2018.

Wikipedia contributors. "Josephine St. Pierre Ruffin." *Wikipedia, The Free Encyclopedia*. Wikipedia, The Free Encyclopedia, 22 Nov. 2018. Web. 4 Jan. 2019

Wikipedia contributors. "Madam C. J. Walker." *Wikipedia, The Free Encyclopedia*. Wikipedia, The Free Encyclopedia, 23 Dec. 2018. Web. 4 Jan. 2019.

Wikipedia contributors. "Daniel Hale Williams." *Wikipedia, The Free Encyclopedia*. Wikipedia, The Free Encyclopedia, 13 Nov. 2018. Web. 16 Dec. 2018.

Wikipedia contributors. "Carter G. Woodson." *Wikipedia, The Free Encyclopedia*. Wikipedia, The Free Encyclopedia, 2 Jan. 2019. Web. 7 Jan. 2019.

Winter, Kari J. "Smith, James McCune (1813-1865)." *BlackPast.org* Remembered & Reclaimed. 2017. Web. 5 Dec. 2018.

www.ingramcontent.com/pod-product-compliance
Lightning Source LLC
Chambersburg PA
CBHW060820090426
42738CB00002B/49